# DATE DUE

| | | | |
|---|---|---|---|
| | | | |
| | | | |
| | | | |
| | | | |
| | | | |
| | | | |
| | | | |
| | | | |
| | | | |
| | | | |
| | | | |
| | | | |
| | | | |
| | | | |
| | | | |
| | | | |
| | | | |

Demco, Inc. 38-293

NOV 1 3 2009

MEAN

PHOENIX **POETS**

# mean

## COLETTE LABOUFF ATKINSON

THE UNIVERSITY OF CHICAGO PRESS *Chicago and London*

COLETTE LABOUFF ATKINSON is associate director of
the International Center for Writing and Translation at the
University of California, Irvine.

The University of Chicago Press, Chicago 60637
The University of Chicago Press, Ltd., London
© 2008 by The University of Chicago
All rights reserved. Published 2008
Printed in the United States of America
17  16  15  14  13  12  11  10  09  08      1  2  3  4  5

ISBN-13: 978-0-226-03057-9 (cloth)
ISBN-13: 978-0-226-03059-3 (paper)
ISBN-10: 0-226-03057-1 (cloth)
ISBN-10: 0-226-03059-8 (paper)

Library of Congress Cataloging-in-Publication Data
Atkinson, Colette LaBouff.
    Mean / Colette LaBouff Atkinson.
        p. cm. — (Phoenix poets series.)
    ISBN-13: 978-0-226-03057-9 (cloth : alk. paper)
    ISBN-13: 978-0-226-03059-3 (pbk. : alk. paper)
    ISBN-10: 0-226-03057-1 (cloth : alk. paper)
    ISBN-10: 0-226-03059-8 (pbk. : alk. paper)
    I. Title.
PS3601.T4895M43 2008
811'.6—dc22                           2007051716

♾ The paper used in this publication meets the minimum
requirements of the American National Standard for
Information Sciences—Permanence of Paper for Printed
Library Materials, ANSI Z39.48-1992.

*The happiness of being with people.*

—FRANZ KAFKA

*I am not I.*

—SIR PHILIP SIDNEY

# Contents

# *Acknowledgments*

Thanks and acknowledgments are made here to the editors and publications in which these prose poems first appeared in other versions:

*Exquisite Corpse:* "1971"
*Identity Theory:* "Mean" and "Mean, Part Two"

My gratefulness goes first to Killarney Clary, James McMichael, and Peter Lippincott Atkinson for their support, which offered me the ease and discomfort to make these poems possible. I'd also like to acknowledge Ngũgĩ wa Thiong'o, who reminded me that the work week would not make sense without this. Thanks to the good readers: Lorene Delany-Ullman, Patty Seyburn, and Kenneth Young. To my family and also those who go before me, more thanks.

MEAN

# Space Race

I knew him before he was broken. He wanted me and I wanted to break him. And then I wanted him not to want me anymore. And then I wanted him to call. When it happened—all of it in just that order—I drove to his house. We watched the longest movie, *The Right Stuff*, which I had the patience to sit through since I knew at the end we'd have sex. Somewhere in the film, in the middle of an argument about how chasing women who don't matter can ruin everything, Gus Grissom says *The issue here ain't pussy. The issue is monkey.* And that movie watching had nothing to do with space or history or men or monkeys. All he wanted was sex. I'd waited a couple of years for that: to have seen him broken and mended and then looking right through me, right on to the stars. I would still want to mean so little that I'd be see-thru. Sometimes I can daydream him back to breakable. Mostly, I would want to watch movies with him while he's in love with someone else and helping himself to me.

# Mean

Wife two was a stripper. And sweet, as well. He traded her in for me. To people I don't know, I say she was a dancer. I watch them, puzzled, wonder how anyone could not love a ballerina. And you have to question a guy like that: trading in a sweet stripper for me. Not a homemaker. Not home much at all. Not sweet. More like my grandfather, Jimmy Grieco. Mean. My mother likes to describe the blue-sky day when she bought me a helium balloon and I let it go. I was six. I begged for another. She said, *okay, but, if you let this one go, I'm really going to be mad*. I nodded, took the string in my hand, held tight, and then opened my hand flat so the balloon lifted and its string slipped up and away. *You were never sweet*, my mother says.

\* \* \*

In Vegas, a few weeks ago, Jimmy and I sorted photographs in his double-wide just off Boulder Highway. My mother stood on the sidelines. She hates how I ask Jimmy for the hard stories. Tell me about the moonshine. Tell me about the dead kids. Tell me how your mother saved the family by burning down the farm. Jimmy's crooked finger points to a picture of the family. That was Leonard. *He was deaf and dumb.* Died at twelve. That was Vincent. *The baby who fell off the staircase without a rail.* Dead at two. Then there's his mother, surrounded by her children. *She was tough,* he says. *Tough.* When Chicago's Black Hand demanded ten thousand dollars, she stuffed five grand in her apron, grabbed my grandfather—then five—and took him to deliver the money. *That's all you'll ever get*, she said, *and don't touch my kids or I'll kill you.*

\* \* \*

My grandfather never asks about the first or second wife. I don't have to tell him that ballerina-fable. He knows I'm three and mean. He knows it for his whole life. His first, my grandmother, was like sugar. He burned her, abandoned her in LA, raced to Mexico, paved road turning to dirt; he ate prickly pear, maybe, on the way to his quick divorce. And, though he won't tell this story, his own father lived, first, with a sweet woman on a wheat farm, far south in Craco, Italy. He boarded a ship, told his wife he'd send for her, and then fled to New York. And in an apartment on Mulberry Street, he met up with the new girlfriend and they disappeared into their new world. She wasn't pretty. *She was tough*. She got busted twice for making moonshine. Her sons loved her. She was mean.

# *Mean, Part Two*

Wife one was a child-bride. He introduced her to me in Greenport, New York, eight years ago. She wore her black skirt the same length I wore mine. A woman like that, who covers her legs, likes to hide. Right away, she told me she was always torn over work. Told me how she cried her eyes out years earlier when, divorced, she had to leave her baby for a long day away. By then, she'd been left for wife two.

And you have to wonder about a guy like that: trading in his child-bride, leaving his son and newborn, for another. But we skipped over that part of the yarn and didn't stop to speculate. Besides, it would have been disloyal. She asked: *Where'd you get those shoes?* Later, I sent her some fabric for a cushion. She dug a chair out of the trash, varnished it, recovered it, brought it to me whole and new. I stopped by her house for tea. She came to a barbeque to celebrate my first anniversary. We roasted pig. *Where'd you get that skirt?* I asked. She sent me postcards and recipes for bisque. Thanked me for taking care of her son in California. Once she flew here with her youngest, a girl. We went to the beach. Got burned.

Two years ago, I went to New York and we did the city museums. On the first floor of the Met, like a docent, she led me through the armor: *The boys always loved this part.* It was still magical, you could tell, not the armor, not the shield of King Henry II of France, its battle scene intertwined with the story of his marital wars. Just a memory of boys looking at gold-gilt or dreaming. For the afternoon, we were at home among steel, brass, and iron. If things were difficult as a child-bride, you'd be surprised how much wife one doesn't let on. If things were ever rough for me, I'd be hard-pressed to complain to her. We're both loyal, after all. We learned it late. Better just to know it: who he is, how we were both mean to wife two, how, if you saw the length we wore our skirts and heard us talk over lunch, you'd wonder who on earth we were.

# Medium Intense Red Copper

At the hair salon I swept floors. Answered phones. Got my hair colored weekly: deep reds, black. Before a trip to Mexico, I bleached it Barbie-white. My father said I looked like Eartha Kitt. A hairdresser I met asked if I'd let her cut my hair and, on the spot, I moved to her side of the salon. The guy who'd been cutting my hair for years didn't mind. Besides, everyone could see she made me look better, like a girl. I got to know her enough to beg her for more: a deep conditioning. Straightening. Just a few lowlights. What I should have said was *please turn me into someone I'm not*. Just the way Eartha Kitt sang in 1954: *And whatever I've got I'm eager to lose*. Or, please turn me into someone I'd like to be. Like Catwoman. The hairdresser knew what I meant. She'd grown up on Catalina Island— where the world was doll-like—and married her school-sweetheart before she preferred girls. She and I drove across town and to bars. We danced, and I was masquerading in whatever new color I'd barely washed out. She was pretending to be someone not interested in me. Her forearms were always stained with the tint.

# Rocket

*Dead Calm* had been advertised in the trailers with phrases like *A voyage into fear. High Seas. Deep terror. Try to stay calm.* In that movie, a couple takes a trip after the violent death of their child only to find, in the middle of the ocean, a maniac. But the wife, Rae, even if she is grieving, saves her husband and gets the killer, too. I was on my way to the movie because I was a flirt, which meant trying to look good and something as shallow as hoping I'd be someone he'd see again. On the highway back from dinner, yellow and blue tile on brick. A white light display. Things shine nights like that. In the heart of Laguna, a stoplight. Coming soon, like high seas, would be a big drop into nothing—chiffon— where I would nod and talk, but mostly keep track of his desire. Did he like me more? Did I make his world wide? The minute I thought he might like me less things would be over. But I plunged in. Like the baby who rockets out the car windshield in the film's opening scene.

# *Loose*

Between the good days and what came next, I made a point of getting him
to a party where I would be star for a half hour. I didn't care that he was still
interested in me or that he might not have wanted to be somewhere to see I
hadn't meant the invitation to be a door to anything. I was just glad to have him
there. Like decoration. A hummingbird feeding in my courtyard: a pulsing,
intense center in my scene. I talked to everyone but him, whom I avoided
because he wanted something—I wasn't sure what—that I would never give.
Especially because he wanted it. Especially because he meant well. When he
wanted to talk about this, I stomped and left. Drove a direction I told him I
wouldn't. *Fuck him*, I thought, *if he wants to watch me run.* And saying this
hardened me. *Fuck him*, I thought, again. Saying this turned me to stone; I drove
south to hide out with someone else. Dug my nails into my legs until they bled.
Remembered the day I loosed a young cat into a field because I figured she, like
me, could make it in the grass on her own. *Stone.* Who could want that?

# Heat Wave

The Garnet Market for candy from the Korean couple who ran the store. Two more blocks and a right at South Lucia Avenue and Wendy climbed the hill to Prospect. But first we would have to pass the stretch of rentals. And I tried to rush, but I don't know why. At one apartment, there was a garden of weeds, surfboard in the dirt, a door opened. A man, long-haired and tired, walked out into the sun. He looked at Wendy and me and then only at me. *Hey, little girl. I want your soul*, he said and then seemed sucked back into the house behind his door. Wendy started to laugh. I ran. My soul. His want. Linda Ronstadt crackled from my bedside radio. *Burnin' in my heart.* He was coming for me.

# Hart Crane Slept Here

Each morning, downward, Maria Stella Maris Church glows out the passenger-side window. Further, the corner where the Salvation Army stood and Hart Crane spent the night. At a shore-edge bar, where they'd finally met up, they shared bottles, walked out toward being together, a hotel, and then got rolled. Crane spent the night in the shelter. E., bruised, shipped out the next morning. The hungover poet took the train back toward Altadena. From my car, not much has changed; I see young stevedores shrug off last night's drunk. Past New Dock Street, a cigarette splits, balloons into orange under my wheels. Hot ash. My unkindness is thrown over and over. Door to door, a ride is for what I've squirreled away, not riches but a pile: the ways no thing mattered, how a kiss didn't count, how a friendship could be severed by a coyote walking between us or a dream. My windshield is a tracery. Long ago, down Gaffey, we raced in my hairdresser's sports car. She drove with her knees. Her perfume, the want, filled the heated car. We drove once to her husband's parking lot, switched cars—he'd shipped out for days—and toured in his jeep. But in this home I've chosen, there's a church on every corner and mourners in between. Boys pair up and nothing happens. Girls hold hands. We get rolled. They ship out. Liquor is drained. The train returns to Altadena. Mary, star of the sea, watches over the gem of a filthy port like the hawk, diamond-shaped ahead. She lets me pass five days a week. On my way uphill there are ovals of golden light, then no one home. Shoeless child, chimes, and stevedore off work. Burnt lawn. Hellhole. Haven. Next stop, my house.

# *Four*

Angry, I came home talking about Tasha. She'd been following me through the sandbox, across blacktop, all the way to our desks. She wanted me to be friends with her only. I'd been stretching my circle further at the preschool where I cut shapes and named clouds. Lately, I had been hanging around the boy with the stitches in his finger. Tasha wanted me to stop, and, when I didn't, she followed me down the slide, into the barrels, onto a swing. *She won't leave me alone,* I told my mother. *I'll be Tasha,* my mother said, *and you be you. Practice,* she encouraged me, *telling her to go away.* My mother followed me room to room around the small house twice. I said *this is silly.* Pretending to be myself.

# London (1987)

Coldest winter days in its recorded history. After Elvis Costello at the Royal Albert Hall, I made my way downstairs to a café. Ordered a drink. I asked for it. *This ruins people*, I thought, thirsty. And The Cure sang *show me, show me, show me* in their sad mascara longing. In the London dungeon, I looked for someone to run with, too. I was good for running. In my own way—inside—just ruined.

# *Wrecking*

We ate, maybe. We might have seen a movie. Later, there was a Southern California warm breeze we'd grown up with coming through. He showed me a photograph of him eating flapjacks in Santa pajamas. I slept hard into white sunlight. When I woke, I didn't know what to do. Picked up my clothes. Knocked the foot of the bed. Told him I'd call him. Or asked him to call. I was beginning, then, to get ahead. As if it had been a race. I took the keys and drove out of the city founded as a temperance colony where, later, there was a goldfish farm and then a mall built over that. Perfect streets. Perfect like someone else. I drove as fast as I could. I could feel it, too: drive-in, farmland, aircraft, sugar beets, goldfish, a film of myself. My past behind me. A blur on the best morning. Drive fast. Be steadfast. Use it wisely. Feel the earth beneath. Wood pulp. Don't return calls. Don't go back. Get drunk. Don't get undressed. Be sweet. Apologize. If you need demolition, use it. Skilled powdermen don't die. At the end of the workday, the best are bone-tired.

# Three Days of the Condor

Because he takes Kathy Hale. Ties her up. He's in the CIA. Someone's trying to kill him. He needs time to sort things out. You'd think she'd panic more, but she doesn't. Would give anything to be spared having to go to the mountains where the boyfriend, Ben, is waiting in Vermont. He's nothing now that she's sleeping next to Joe Turner, who's just threatened her. He needs some shut eye. And *the night is still young*. She's less interested in running. When the guy dressed as a mailman goes after Turner, Hale gets in on the action. Finds a carving knife. That's her man. Blond hair and sweatered. A Doxa sharkhunter watch. Under the umbrella of his drama, she never notices her hands are still bound. Forgets to ask to be released. She'll help him. However she can. I'm no Kathy Hale, but I love bookish Joe Turner. And not because he's got an exciting life. But because he'll erase mine and make me the *'ol spyfucker* he can count on. A kind of prisoner to something larger. After years together, he'd still ask me: *do you know **anybody** that well?*

# The Glass Show Lounge

I'm looking for Juju, my great-uncle, dead since 1984. He shot himself in Hollywood, Florida.

But no one is talking.

The closest I get is someone remembers a neon sign—a face and cigar in lights. One dancer in aquamarine pasties. Or pictures with him at Leavenworth. I find a musician in Chicago who remembers Juju and *The Glass Show Lounge*. He pretends to give me the straight story, clears his throat: *Well, he was a fair gangster*. But he mostly wants to talk about piano, the old days. *There was a Polish singer there who had real pipes*. He tries to dredge her name. Instead, he sings. *My old flame, I can't even think of his name / But it's funny now and then / how my thoughts go flashing back again / to my old flame*. He remembers the singer while he stands at the hallway pay phone in Chicago. He tries to be standup, says he's been away and would like to get back, get a gig. He's just as lost as I am: *Do you know where I can get a gig? Can you help me?* In one letter's postscript, he reassures me: *Juju died of self-inflicted gunshot wounds due to lung cancer*. I can tell what he's saying: *He was dead already*. The musician's good-guy show falls away: *Blew his head off. That guy had the nerve.*

# Bakasana

Yesterday, the teacher said we would try Bakasana again. *Crow*, he said. I moved as he directed. Hands planted, leaning forward with my face toward the ground. *Think about what a crow is like*, he said. *It's okay to fall*. I moved and thought: crows don't fall. I leaned until I stood on my two arms. Myself invisible to me. *I'll count to five*, he said, and, because I couldn't last that long, I thought of arguing with my mother. She'd said *don't you always feel sorry for the crows? They're so black and ugly. What about the blue and gloss?* I'd asked. Or their focus? How gorgeous: not to know how one looks.

# Deal

*If you shut up until we get there, I'll buy your favorite perfume,* he offered. *Hermes? Fracas?* I asked. *Just stop talking.* I wanted a new scent. He wanted quiet. Sometimes, I think of that, being bought out of what I want to say because I want something else. Herodotus winds through stories of women like this. When, at a banquet, the Egyptian, Sesostris, and his family are trapped in a house set on fire, he turns to his wife and asks what to do. She tells him to take two of their sons— there were six—and stretch them over the flames. Build a bridge for the rest. He did this. Burning his kids. Making a path with flesh. *Treading on them*, Herodotus says. Because that wife wanted some saved. Wanted other things I don't know. To end the evening walking from a burning house.

# "I'm sorry I was blind"

On the way to Bishop Montgomery High School in 1982, the car radio played only top 40 hits and traffic alerts. Willie Nelson was singing Elvis Presley, a sadder version: *Always on My Mind* was flattened into a crossover smash. Its refrain was followed by phrases that made me suspicious: *maybe I didn't love you as well as I should have.* My mother, bracing herself for the workday, asked: *do you think it's enough?* We were stopped in an intersection. *To say "you were always on my mind?"* I remember thinking *I'm supposed to say no, say it should never be enough.* I should want more.

# *Hover*

Heard his skateboard with its rickety crackle. He cornered at Vincent Street. Leaned in and his beach-white hair covered his face. We called him Charlie, then. I was ten and, with Elaine, watched from my front porch across the street. When I was twenty-five, we called him Chuck. He drove a 1971 Corvette at the tail end of its chrome days. Nevada Silver. Hard and shiny. I heard the 350 corner at Vincent. Watched his sandy hair fall. I could tell—even from my vantage point—he was drunk and had taken Valium. That he was torn about quitting. Something in how he slammed his car door. Red eyed, I walked across the street.

# Intention (The Dead Leaves)

To have the week make sense, my mother took us to the Old Towne Mall for an ice cream, running down my hand, or a ride on the carousel. Horses almost what they should be. In school, I learned later that it didn't matter what the novelist intended. His story was what it was. Larger. Smaller than he wanted. *Today is going to be a good day* ends up being a ridiculous wish. At night, again, it's what I wanted to have done. Or said. How it didn't come out the way I thought. How it was worse. Or could be more beautiful and, if I hadn't planned that, I won't correct anyone. Upstairs, at work, someone plays "Autumn Leaves." Thirty versions. Johnny Mercer's words. Original French. Chanson. Jazz. A capella. Guitar. Thirty tries, a broken record of regret. All day, November appears as July, lost: *the sunburned hands I used to hold.* That someone wanted to keep holding a hand and can't. Whatever I want *now* to be, it's something else. If I mean to find a way out down a big dirt trail, it's a wood platform. A pink and grey filly in circles.

# Gain

My great-uncle Joe wrote the column for the ILWU Warehouse News under a pseudonym, Tyrone Gillespie. Between the lines, *be wise—organize*—he wrote the union workers' news straight from Thrifty Drug Warehouse: *And the hungry men from Thrifty Drug came through with flying colors. They needed three out of three from the league leading Hollywood Loomcraft team to take the bowling championship. And they did it.* He refers to himself—a trophy-holding member of the winning bowling team—as one of the *Hawthorne Whiz Kids.* His column details climate conditions in the warehouse. The way the higher-ups speak to employees. The personal news: *Eloise out sick. Adele has had an operation. One man's daughter has been made a queen.* There's a piece on what the Thrifty workers are reading in April 1952: *Childhood and Adolescence, How to Bake a Cake, What to Do Until the Doctor Comes, My Gun is Quick* and *Vengeance is Mine.* He was a reader and writer, too. About that time, at home, he was developing television ideas from lessons he'd sent away for. His assignments included writing a fairy tale from the past, a how-to-do-it program. His fairy tale, *The Golden Pony,* was unfinished but typed. *I wished for hands of gold,* one of the characters said. He wished, I could tell, and began and began the fairy tale with *A small boy . . .* On the backside of one draft, he kept minutes from a union meeting: *what will you gain? How best to maintain a strong bargaining position? The company's shooting for a settlement of 6 to 8 cents.* And again, *what will you gain?* It's clear he thought nothing was fair. He was cold in the warehouse, had a small bedroom in Hawthorne, California, and, at night, he dreamed a gold TV pony.

# Spring Fling

In the dressing room next to mine, two girls. They're trying on prom dresses and go quiet while one shoves the fabric up over herself. Then the gushing—*oh my god, get that one. You have to get it*—comes and a cell phone rings. The girl tells her mother she's found two. But I know what the mother wants to ask: *does the dress make you look like a whore?* The girl talks back about the cost and prom and the boy that the girls want to visit later. A salesgirl comes to ask if I need help. *Can I get you another size?* I tell her no. *I'm finished here.* I always am. It's midday in Newport Beach. I gather zeros and extra smalls. My shape fit for a schoolgirl's uniform. But the size of a schoolgirl. Not a woman dressing up as one. Nothing fits. No jeans. Low-cut sweater. Plunging neckline or knee-length hem. It's not the clothes. It's that you haven't yet grown into the world. What it wants from you. When I was in the eighth grade, Sister Dennis Anne screamed at me for not wearing a bra when we were learning the fox-trot in the parish hall. I had a body, a way of hiding, which forgave such a mistake. The prom-dress girls spill out their stalls. Fit the earth.

# New World

Pointing to a drawing—it was a man's head, neck, and shoulders—my father said *this man hurts people*. I don't think he said *murder* and I know he didn't say *rape*. I am sure, too, that I didn't ask him to explain. I saw beyond the table to the carpet and out the window to the pale green Volkswagen. He kept the lesson short; *if a stranger tries to take you, do not go.* My father meant well when he showed me a composite sketch of a serial rapist and stranger. I was five. What could he do? How would it hurt? What I could understand I let stand in for the rest: *be afraid of what you do not know.* My father ate his toast and bacon and said I had to eat mine.

# *Laurel*

Marriage began in New York where we hadn't lived before. He was out. Sometimes on a sailboat with his brothers. I was inside reading and with his mother who first could no longer put words together and then could not speak. Sometimes she would go out and sit in the convertible. Ready to go.

At the end of the day, I would ask—or thought I did—*what's it like out there? How long is the boat? What did you have for lunch?* But these questions didn't interest me or anyone else. And, while the woman—it was dusk, summer—fell away from us, I heard her breathing. I saw a cardinal.

# Replacement Monkey

They were eighteen. She asked him for a horse. If she'd wanted a baby, she didn't know it. *A horse.* He never understood that meant *take me from the city.* Instead, he settled on a monkey. She called him Joey. Sitting on her head, Joey loved her, brushed back her blond hair, wouldn't leave her. He told me how he tried to give her a break from the monkey, buckled Joey into the car's front seat, carted him to work—a construction site—and played classical music to keep the beast calm. Back home, Joey tore the stuffing from the sofa and then, when he was quarantined to the bathroom—a kind of makeshift cage—he shredded the shower curtain, rug, and walls. He shaved his own belly. Squeezed out the toothpaste. She begged to have him returned to the exotic pet store. *What she really wanted was a horse. I packed for the country and we drove to Virginia.* Easy to see how someone might fall for this story, a romance. Imagining her not knowing what she wanted. Imagining her wanting a horse. Imagining him wanting to make up for what she could not have. The woman asks for too much. And the man, straining to understand, offers her all the wrong things.

# *Spirit*

I don't recall the gift, attached to the unsent postcard. Its white space was filled
with the tiny, sideways scrawl of a left-handed writer. The first line said *this
girl reminds me of you* and sounded heartbroken. I flipped the card to find—in
black and white—a bust. An incredible raven-haired woman. Her head was
thrown back. Her neck exposed. She was not embarrassed by how pleased she
was. She was motionless and the photographer probably didn't ever have to
ask her to stay *like that. Right there.* I wanted to leave those moments. So it was
nearly impossible to turn the card over and keep reading. I was none of these
things: still or fit for a framed view. I didn't even know what color my hair really
was. He had misunderstood. *This picture reminds me of you* should have been
paired with —on the flip side—a Technicolor version of Northrop's B-2 Stealth
Bomber. It debuted in the late eighties with weight and a purpose to destroy.
About the time I stopped seeing him.

# *Proximity*

In the parking space, a sparrow. Sitting. Could I see his heart beat? When I bent down, he tried to fly. No luck with a broken wing. Feathers spreading, he screamed, spun onto his back, convulsed, and—one leg up, then the other—died. In the parking lot of Fashion Island, fake tits and whitened teeth and lots of lazy laughter passed me by. Sparrow's gone. As if nature is natural. For some time now, I've been hot on the heels of this. A sparrow without a chance. Handfuls of wanting. Handfuls of nothing. Meanwhile, dogs are digging up Hoffa.

# *Juju's Sister*

From Vegas, my grandfather yells: *if you want to know about your great-uncle Juju, call your Aunt Margaret, my sister, in Florida.*

She barks: *why do you want to know about this?* I don't want to answer; I see the conversation will be a standoff. I know I've called the right place. We're clearly related. I ask instead about the ocean. My great-aunt Margaret is eighty-four, blind, with a heavy voice. Though Juju's been dead over twenty years, she's his sister and not herself. Still, she's the keeper of his things.

# *G u n   D o g*

*A good thing to learn*, he says. My new neighbor, Bob, says he'll tell me how to shoot. *Especially for a young woman*. Alone. And even though I told my husband I wanted a divorce, he armed me with advice up to the last minute: *if someone comes into your house, hide the gun. Surprise him. Do you know how to sharpen knives? And tell me: what do you do if you get accosted on a street*. This is the help I get after deciding to live alone at thirty-nine. I need weapons. A Smith and Wesson Centennial Airweight (I can handle the kick). A poker face. Plenty of room.

# *Flower Girl*

Slightly too old for it. But small enough. My sister and I wore pink dresses. Everyone looked at her. She danced with the most beautiful man there. I danced with the other adults. My parents had just split up, and this was my first wedding. At the Biltmore Hotel, in a suite the night before, my aunt fought with her husband-to-be about something unimportant and then, while mad, ruined her manicure—an acrylic nail—with a cigarette. Spiraling out of the underground lot in downtown LA afterward, my sister leaned, left and right, to The Eagles. *Hopeless romantics, here we go again.*

# Park Bench

*Don't ever do that to me again*, I said, as if one could ask for things not to happen and, at the same time, expect to enjoy anything like being together. Because what could being together mean except moving, unaware of rules? And when he agreed, I heard his *okay,* flat if loving. Was I pleased? As glad as whining Catherine in *Jules and Jim*: *You said "I love you." I said "wait" I was going to say "take me." You said "go away."* No Jeanne Moreau drama followed. This is done, I thought, and then kept enjoying the sun.

Not everyone's ready to drive a car off the pier.

# "Perhaps this verse would please you better — Sue — (2)"

Before boys, Susan drove me to work, for teriyaki takeout on Manchester past Lincoln Boulevard. Inseparable, we planned winter and Easter vacations. In the stairwell, I tried to talk. She cut me off. Her echo was loud when she said *you can't see yourself.* We went to see *Purple Rain*. That fall, I had dinner with a boy. Susan was angry and told me I was wrong. I felt it was true. Was it *that* boy? That he had once dated someone Susan knew? We stopped talking. We were eighteen. A decade later, I turned a corner coming out of a bookstore and heard Susan laugh. *I know that*, I thought, remembering how she'd saved me from saying who I was. I circled back. She answered as she had before we fell out. She answered with shame. *Do you remember how things ended*, she asked, *because of boys?*

# Prosthetic

She had wanted to move to the country and he had tried to please her. She'd
asked for a life in Virginia but now she'd need to wait. They'd gotten a
broken-down car he needed to fix. She read books, hoped by Saturday they'd
leave. Sunday came and he was still down in the street. Tools in hand.
Three-day-old clothes. He told this story about their past and focused mostly,
in the telling, on the car. He couldn't see the leaving. Only saw the fixing. But
the day did come. He unlocked the passenger-side door. She screamed *it's a
leg,* and he reached for the flesh-colored prosthetic leg they found between the
front seats. *Weird*, he said, tapping it. She gagged. Throwing the leg onto the
sidewalk, he said *there. Let's go.* But she wouldn't move, wouldn't get in the car,
wouldn't leave for Virginia. It was bad luck. The truth is she would never have
gone.

# Garden Variety

The spiders seemed really hungry so I cupped brown butterflies. Fed them into webs. Pinned wings in my fingers, the Fiery Skippers strained, and their struggle might have sounded like Cicero to the Senate: *why is this my fate?* He began against Marc Antony with that vague question. But what was *this*? Forming sentences? Telling his long story? His severed head and hands on the rostra? In the garden, I didn't feel any questions flutter in my hands. I didn't think of it as killing butterflies that covered the lantana and grass. What I did notice: there were fewer spiders. And why should they wait so long, still and splayed, for luck?

# "For God's sake, get out"

We were into horror, what we learned to talk about like it was real: the devil. That he'd been something else, Lucifer, before. I had begged my father to take me. *The Amityville Horror* was playing and everyone in my Catholic school would see it. That night, in the bed, I woke my father every hour. Would he look out the window to see? He said *it's just the wind*. I remember wanting to say that sounded like a line from a scary movie, but that I was still afraid of whatever was coming. Not knowing what to say. Wanting not to sound like a crazy child. Someone in the movie had said *houses don't have memories*. Still, when we moved into our house I could smell the fabric of the sewing room where the woman had worked and where I now slept. And dirt on the back porch where her husband took off his work boots.

# *Route*

The turkey vultures spent nights on the Light of Christ, a Lutheran Church and
preschool where they'd line up for sleep. They were chased away, probably by
the pastor, who worried about the message they'd send: *death and carnage here!*
How misunderstood. Still, no one wants to think about how, with blood-red
heads, they eat the dead. Ugly stepsisters of the Condors, the vultures moved
up the road. They come home now the same time I do. Black and circling, they
linger for updrafts, wait for permission. Sometimes I wait for the green and
like the idling exhaust, a dead stop. At Culver and Michelson, the birds, coming
from the south, circle and circle on thermals and make a hard left. I make a
right; the sun, its light now losing, backs me. We cross each other; they bow
and I stretch up. Flying reminders of the fifth commandment, they're in sight
of three gum trees where Culver meets Sandburg. Over condos and traffic and
golf, they—black hearts—face the ocean. They never glance back at their old
home. Even if they were able to reflect, what's to consider? There's nothing
savage in them. At home, I pull my windblown hair into a knot. It's dusk. We
tuck our heads into pillows, wings.

# *1652*

I'll go and then I won't. Dana Point for shorebirds. Kite-flying in Palos Verdes. The Sierras in October. Sunday in Santa Monica. The same bookstore for the hundredth time. I can't say what happens between what I have to give and having seen agreement go. In Playa del Rey, a hand on my knee. I remember thinking it wasn't that I didn't want him, but I couldn't help myself, anyway, from saying *I have to read Milton now*. Because I knew we'd never get anywhere together. Because I was thinking about 1652. What kind of year that might have been for John Milton. Death of a wife and child. Birth of a child. Blindness. How he had to carry on deep into those months as if he had not been able to see when the new year had turned.

# Graphic Novel Romance (V for Vendetta)

After he brains a fingerman, V drops his baton and tells Evey he means her no harm. *Who are you?* she asks. *What I am is a man in a mask.* Later, she wakes up in his cave. Stan Getz plays. V hums along, makes her hole-in-bread for breakfast. In the theater, I lean over to my friend. *This is how I got married.* I was taken, I like to say. It wasn't a cave. But "The Girl from Ipanema" played. Coffee was made. Books were everywhere and in alphabetical order. He split cantaloupe so I didn't have to use a knife. And I said *who are you?* He answered: *I've forgotten more than you've ever known.* With the film still running, my friend reminds me *this is comic book stuff.*

# Ghost Squad

I walk to pinball machines. He steers me to big displays, lights, and handheld weapons. I don't want to play. *This way, you'll like this,* he promises like he knows me. We stand in front of Sega's Ghost Squad. A light-gun game. I can go single, three-shot, or—my choice—fully automatic. The voiceover says I should prepare to be part of a special forces unit. We're elite. Three missions: Air Force One, Grand Villas, or Jungle. We choose our mini-drama—Grand Villas— where we'll save the president and summit leaders. He shoots bad guys. I shoot hostages. It's an accident, but he says *you meant to do that, didn't you?* When the game ends, I'm disappointed. He's laughing: *you didn't get much, did you?* I agree and then think, *no, but I got you once.* He says more: *look at my score. Look at yours.* And I nod but think I've known him long enough to remember the time he brought me flowers and I wasn't home to get them. A lot of shooting and no one goes down. Thank god for the arcade noise and missed opportunities. I remember the dank games room at the pier when I was ten where I'd go after I had lost—I thought it was my fault—chances to catch bonito at sunrise.

I guide us over to skeeball. Cracking and rolling and wood I can wish on.

# Hips

The last thing we want to think about. My aunt is divorced and moving to a smaller house. My cousin, eleven, stands near the heated pool; a hula hoop circles her straight waist. We clear the garage, find a box of my grandmother's papers and there, a scrapbook, bound and handmade. Color paper is pasted with poems she copied and pictures of Hollywood movie stars. Gable. Women swooning. Above one couple, she's written *Is this love?* Over her favorite, dark-haired Kay Francis and William Powell, the handwriting is sure. She must've known *One Way Passage*: the dying beauty finds love with a criminal on the Pacific. At sea, even a match like that would last. Did she remember the film's end when she asked the same question on every page? My aunt digs to the bottom of the box. My cousin begs me to play, throws a hoop over my neck. *There's nothing to it*, I tell her. Nothing compared to asking *is this love?* Holding the ticking ring high.

# *1971*

Mt. Rainier in front of my summer hair looked almost paper-thin. We'd come that far: my aunt's black car crowded with women and children. They drove to show us something besides the wait for Friday night's facedown cards and smoke in their low-hanging kitchen lights. Four of us fit around them, women who lorded over two motel queens the first night.

When the road opened, we stopped for Lee, carsick. I leaned on the hot fence, plastic bags banging there. Later, Neil and Bobby waded into a lake and came out screaming, drawing in the air a snake they'd seen. Further north, at a café, we talked with a tall man whose leg, an open sore, was crossed for me to watch. He pointed out leaves to avoid. Everything green could hurt me. On the last day before we turned the car south, my mother asked a ranger about a bear we'd seen the year before. *Shot*, he said.

But no one wanted to return. And no one noticed the men were gone until the 101 and somewhere near the Santa Susanna Pass. The black Impala, lost in the Ventura night, strayed. I heard them say this is where it happened. I heard them, in the front seat, say let's sing a song. The too-thick gap between words forced me to the floor. They sang. I listened to the engine. Between songs, my aunt couldn't see a goddamn thing.

# Port of Los Angeles

I'd have given the quarters, but the organ-grinder's monkey took them from me. He, who'd be going away, watched from the shade. *You looked afraid of the monkey in the dress*, he laughed. We passed coral on glass shelves. In Ports O' Call Village, maritime themes were everywhere. But especially this: departures and arrivals. Families cracked crab. Spilled butter. Excess and good time coming. Packing the car and squeezing back in. Going home. Far. I never cried for anyone who left. Instead, for the dead great blue heron in the street. Augustine, over the loss of his closeness with God, said *I didn't weep for this, but instead I wept for Dido who surrendered her life to the sword.* I read that and cry for Augustine, weeping. For Dido watching Aeneas leave. Fleet of loss. Pieces worth twenty-five cents.

# "Taking it like a little soldier, aren't you?"

That part of youth passed, a classroom tick tock, as if not at all. In Buena Park, my cousins wrapped me in a blanket to get me into Knott's Berry Farm for free. *Be quiet*, they said, *you're a baby*. I wanted to be old enough to pay what I owed. When I was twenty-one, I told a woman I wished I had hands like hers. *You don't know what you're asking*, she scolded. A few years later, my hands looked like hers. Shortly after, I married and was still me: feeling inappropriate. Lacking empathy. Now, half-done. Half-baked. I hate the traffic made worse by street slurry work. At home, no one has called for three days. The power's gone out and the microwave's clock is full of zeros. Blinking. Last spring, I spent a whole morning saving a rabbit with a leg so smashed I'm sure it was put down on arrival at the vet. I thought, once or twice, I'd have children. But the doctor says it's *going, going, gone*. Moments now like some bizarre auction. *And that possibility is sold to the woman in the back of the room*. Being me means taking it *smack in the teeth*. Not wanting what she's bought.

# *Fortune-Telling*

*You're the kind of man no one should marry,* I said. *Better to be friends with you.* It was bold and rude, I know, but I said it while we ate ice cream in sugar cones, and king palms, like the melting stuff, waved down. Still, I married him, and years later, we drove through Boise, Idaho. Off the highway, a large green sign said BIRDS OF PREY. Below that, in smaller letters: SCENIC ATTRACTION. I turned and pointed. *Hey, what about that?* But he'd seen *scenic attraction* and had sped ahead. We had a good day, anyway. Montaigne said of his friend that *if you press me to tell you why I loved him, I feel that this cannot be expressed, except by answering: because it was he, because it was I.* Because I wanted to see Cooper's Hawks, their eye sockets stuffed with cotton. Because he did, too, but kept driving.

# Gardena Freeway, California

Artesia Boulevard takes me to my father's old house, past my sister's school. Past the old boyfriend's house. It sees me all the way to 30th Street—sand—where I lived in Hermosa Beach for three years. I take it west. Toward fog or mist or damp air. Driving past Blossom, Felton, Green, I see El Indio Mexican Restaurant and a sign that says "since 1960." If I'm with my mother, she'll always tell me how she and my father, way back, ate there. Every block, each signal stalls me. But I get to see the boulevard: *Mattresses for Sale*, a store that sells sheepskins, a Goodwill. Signal after signal, I move west through Torrance, Redondo Beach, Manhattan Beach, and into Hermosa. On this street, once, I was twenty-two. Riding in a truck with a boyfriend I didn't much like. At Aviation Boulevard, not far from the shore, he asked what in the world I was doing with him. I looked out the windshield, told him I wasn't so interested in him—really—but that I didn't want to see him with the blonde nineteen-year-old who sold Chanel and wrapped her hair atop her head with a single pencil. He was silent, but he might as well have screamed Captain Beefheart: *You used me like an ashtray heart.* He'd have been right. On Artesia, my past is only as rough as selling sheepskin in Santa Ana winds or hawking tacos for close to fifty years. Four lanes help me remember all my hot, wrong words, and then they deliver me to the ocean, too vast for me to hurt.

# *Notes*

The epigraph includes two lines. The first comes from Franz Kafka's diaries, edited by Max Brod and translated by Martin Greenberg with Hannah Arendt. The second is a phrase from sonnet XLV of Sir Philip Sidney's "Astrophel and Stella."

The opening poem contains a line from the film *The Right Stuff.*

In "Mean, Part Two," the work referenced is the *Shield of Henry II of France,* ca. 1555, which is housed at the Metropolitan Museum of Art in New York.

The title "Medium Intense Red Copper" is a L'Oreal hair color and the lyrics are from Eartha Kitt's song "I Want to Be Evil."

"Rocket" references the 1989 film *Dead Calm* and includes trailer lines.

"Heat Wave," both the title and the song's phrase, "Burnin' in my heart," refer to the version that Linda Ronstadt made famous.

"Hart Crane Slept Here" works with an episode Hart Crane details in his letters.

"London (1987)" includes lines from the song "Just Like Heaven" by The Cure.

"Three Days of the Condor" is the title of a film, which starred Robert Redford and Faye Dunaway, who played characters talked about in the poem. Phrases from the film appear in the piece, too.

"The Glass Show Lounge" includes lyrics from the song "My Old Flame" written by Sam Coslow and Arthur Johnston.

"Deal" contains a story and line from Herodotus's *Histories* as translated by David Grene.

"I'm sorry I was blind" is a line from the song "Always on My Mind" as sung by Willie Nelson. The poem also includes the line "maybe I didn't love you as well as I should have."

"Intention (The Dead Leaves)" includes a line from the song "Autumn Leaves."

The title "Spirit" is also the name of the B-2 Bomber.

"Flower Girl" includes the line "Hopeless romantics, here we go again" from The Eagles's "New Kid in Town."

"Park Bench" includes lines from the film *Jules and Jim*.

The title "Perhaps this verse would please you better—Sue—(2)" is a line of a letter from Emily Dickinson to her sister-in-law, Susan Huntington Dickinson; the verse referenced is a version of poem 216, "Safe in Their Alabaster Chambers."

"For God's sake, get out," the title and passage quoted, are lines from the original film version of *The Amityville Horror*.

"Graphic Novel Romance (*V for Vendetta*)" has lines from the film.

"Ghost Squad" is a Sega arcade game, which the poem also describes.

The line about Dido in "Port of Los Angeles" comes from Augustine's *Confessions* as translated by R. S. Pine-Coffin.

The title "Taking it like a little soldier, aren't you?" and the phrase "smack in the teeth" both come from "The Middle or Blue Period," an essay written by Dorothy Parker on her fortieth birthday.

"Fortune-Telling" has a line from Michel de Montaigne's "Of Friendship" as translated by Donald M. Frame.

In "Gardena Freeway, California," the lyrics are from Captain Beefheart's song "Ashtray Heart."